SERIES EDITOR: DONALD SOMMERVILLE

OSPREY MODELLING MANUALS 16

T-34/76 & T-34/85

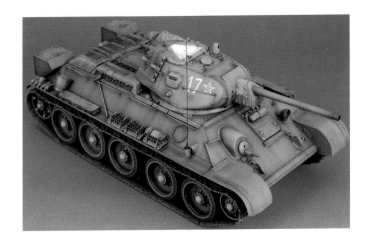

RODRIGO HERNÁNDEZ CABOS

AND

JOHN PRIGENT

OSPREY
MODELLING

First published in Great Britain in 2001 by Osprey Publishing, Elms Court, Chapel Way, Botley, Oxford OX2 9LP United Kingdom
Email: info@ospreypublishing.com

ISBN 1 84176 209 1

Editor: Simon Forty
Design: Compendium Publishing Ltd

Originated by Acción Press, S.A.
Printed in China through World Print Ltd

01 02 03 04 05 10 9 8 7 6 5 4 3 2 1

For a Catalogue of all books published by Osprey Military and Aviation please write to:
The Marketing Manager, Osprey Publishing Ltd., P.O. Box 140, Wellingborough, Northants NN8 4ZA United Kingdom
Email: info@ospreydirect.co.uk

The Marketing Manager, Osprey Direct USA,
c/o Motorbooks International, PO Box 1,
Osceola, WI 54020-001, USA
E-mail: info@ospreydirectusa.com

www.ospreypublishing.com

Acknowledgments

The Introduction and Chapters 3 to 7 were written by John Prigent. The first section of Chapter 1 (T-34/76 Model 1942) was written the step-by-step by Carlos de Diego Vaquerizo; the final section (T-34/76 Model 1943) Jose A. Velázquez Encinas. The first section of Chapter 2 was written by Jordi Escarre; the Model 1943 was written by A. Mayoralas Fernández, the T-34/85 in Croatia is by Miguel Jiménez Martín. The walkround photographs were taken by Rodrigo Hernández Cabos.
Scale Drawings: Carlos de Diego Vaquerizo.
Colour side views: Rodrigo Hernández Cabos.
Model for illustrating the cover: Miguel Jiménez Martín.
Photographs selected by: Accion Press, S.A. ·
The publisher's acknowledge with gratitude the help given by the following museums: Musée des Blindés "Général Estienne" de Saumur, and Bovington Tank Museum.

LEFT **T-34/85 Model 1944 — see pages 40–43.**

CONTENTS

INTRODUCTION

A BRIEF HISTORY OF THE T-34

Before the German invasion of Russia in 1941 there had been a degree of co-operation between the German and Soviet armies. In spite of the mutual hostility of their political creeds, it had suited both Hitler and Stalin to act as allies, most notably in their joint invasion of Poland. Since the early 1930s this co-operation had included the use of Soviet testing grounds to evaluate new German tank designs. German officers had been baffled by their Soviet counterparts' refusal to believe that Germany had nothing better than what was sent for testing.

The T-34 was the reason for this doubt, and it came as an enormous shock to the Germans when they first encountered Russian tank forces during Operation 'Barbarossa'. With its well-sloped armour and potent 76mm armour-piercing gun, the T-34 was more than a match for any of the German tanks. Fortunately for the German tank crews, however, it laboured under several self-inflicted disadvantages. In the first place, Stalin's purges had eliminated many of the Red Army's best tank officers, so tactics were primitive. Secondly, it had a rather unreliable transmission in its early versions and spares were in very short supply. Thirdly, and perhaps most importantly, it had only a two-man turret. The commander acted as gunner as well as directing the driver and, if he was unlucky, trying to command a unit and issue orders to other tanks as well. On top of all this, most tanks lacked radios and orders had

RIGHT **These T-34/76 Model 1943s are seen in winter white, rather crudely applied over their basic green camouflage. The boxes on the hull side of the nearest tank are crates for extra 76mm ammunition, but since they are in such vulnerable positions it seems likely that they are being used to carry the crew's possessions rather than explosive ammunition. Note also the radio aerial and its armoured 'pot' mount.** *via Chris Ellis*

LEFT **Here is a T-34/76 with an alternative type of Model 1943 turret, this one with a flat edge to its lower front. Here you can see the fairly common mixing of roadwheel types which happened when rubber supplies began to run short — all wheels are the perforated ribbed type, but only the front one has a rubber tyre and the others have steel rims. The rear wheel probably had a rubber tyre as well, those wheels being reserved for front and rear positions to cut down the vibrations caused by running on all-steel wheels.** *via Chris Ellis*

to be passed by flag signals. The limited vision afforded by the T-34's large turret hatch which opened forward meant the tank commander had to peer round while exposed to enemy fire: it is hardly surprising that Soviet tank tactics in both attack and defence were somewhat lacking.

Nevertheless the T-34 was a very good tank when properly handled, and later versions proved this as the Red Army drove the Germans back from the outskirts of Moscow to Berlin. The original Model 1940 had a shorter gun than the main production types, mounted in a rounded cast mantlet. A longer gun was soon introduced and remained standard until the 85mm gun became available in 1943. The Models 1941 and 1942 were alike to look at in most respects, but there had been successive internal improvements which gave better engine and transmission reliability as well as a reduced manufacturing time and cost. A cast turret had been developed beside the original welded one, and either could be found on any of the early models.

The Model 1943 used the same hull, but had a new hexagonal turret, seen in several sub-types, which differed mainly in the join between top and bottom sections. The most obviously different was the forged type built at the Chelyabinsk factory, which can be spotted by its rounded top

BELOW **This is a T-34/76 Model 1942 with a cast turret. It has only one stowage bin, unlike the Model 1941, and uses the plain dished roadwheels with rubber tyres which were common in that year. This is a command tank, as can be seen by the radio aerial visible behind the turret; most T-34s at that time had no radios, and those that did had them fitted in the hull with an aerial mount on the right hull side.** *via Chris Ellis*

edge. A vision cupola was introduced part-way through production of the Model 1943.

All the improvements to the T-34 so far had been by slow increments rather than major leaps forward; the Soviet High Command had made a deliberate decision not to allow drastic design changes which might disrupt the production of desperately needed tanks. However, work had been progressing on an improved three-man turret with a vision cupola and a better gun, and the combination was mounted on the original hull to produce the T-34/85. German tanks had improved to the point where the 76mm gun was marginal against many of them, but the new 85mm gun was much more powerful. The new turret also came in several sub-types differing in the details of the join between top and bottom. There is no room here to go into the differences between the sub-types of the T-34/76 and T-34/85: the books suggested in the reference section later deal with them in detail.

Like its predecessors with their 76mm guns, the T-34/85 had several different turret types as variations on the same basic design. The improved tank was a battle-winner against all but the heaviest German tanks, and remained in service long after 1945. Improved versions used a more powerful engine and different roadwheels as well as having internal improvements, and were built in Poland and Czechoslovakia as well as in Russia itself. They were used by the Red Army and its satellites behind the Iron Curtain, of course, but also exported to many countries. T-34/85s were used in the early Middle East Wars, Korea and Vietnam, and are believed to remain in service today with several smaller armies.

MODELLING THE T-34 THEN AND NOW

In the 1960s Revell (the original US company) produced a T-34/85 in about 1/40 scale — opinions still vary about what scale it actually was. It was seen as a good model in its day, and was famously used in a photograph allegedly showing a real T-34 which had rammed a German tank. During the 1970s Tamiya began a small series of T-34 kits, which are still re-released from time to time. They suffered from being

RIGHT **This is another T-34/76 Model 1943. The rubber-tyred, dished roadwheels and infantry grab handles are clearly shown, and this tank carries not only a fuel drum but also a log on its side. The log was not used to fill sunken obstacles but was carried as an undishing aid — if the tank bogged down it could be pushed under the front of the tracks to improve their grip.** *via Chris Ellis*

designed as motorised toys, which meant their hull dimensions were distorted to accommodate the electric motor, gearbox and batteries. However, the distortion is not immediately obvious except to experts and these kits have the advantage that several of the aftermarket companies have produced accessories such as replacement wheel sets specifically to fit the Tamiya kits. A T-34/76

Model 1942 with cast turret was the first kit, followed by a variation with extra parts to produce the version built at Leningrad with appliqué armour added to its hull front and turret, and then by a Model 1943 with its different hexagonal, or six-sided, turret. In 1985 a T-34/85 appeared, and then in the mid-1990s a revision of the T-34/76 Model 1943 to give the drop-forged Chelyabinsk turret type. Unfortunately the opportunity was never taken to revise the hull dimensions and angles for greater accuracy, but the finished models still look like T-34s and are easy to build. Tamiya also produced a T-34/85 in 1/25 scale, which can still be found. Although it shares many of the problems of Tamiya's 1/35 scale T-34s, it is the only kit available in the larger scale.

Meanwhile, several companies had been active in the smaller scales. Airfix produced a 1/76 scale T-34/85, as did Fujimi who also made a T-34/76 with welded turret. Matchbox also made a T-34/76, which is now available from Revell of Germany. Esci produced the T-34/76 Model 1942 with cast turret and the Model 1943, and Bandai gave us two T-34/76s in 1/48 scale.

More recently there has been a minor explosion in 1/35 scale T-34 kits. Dragon's T-34/85 is available as a Model 1944 and as the postwar improved Model 1945, though as yet there is no sign of the T-34/76 kits which had been hoped for. These are excellent models, probably the most accurate ones available. Italeri and Zvezda have produced both T-34/76 and T-34/85 kits, also regarded as very accurate though slightly less easy to build; it is not obvious which company is the original mould-maker for these as they seem to be a co-production.

The position of Eastern European and Russian kit makers, where companies arrive and disappear and trade moulds between themselves, is equally confusing. The same T-34/85 kit has been described as coming from RPM and Maquette, but whoever's box you find it in, it is a good model. It has a different turret type to all the other T-34/85 models, and though the hull angles have the same faults as the Tamiya kits, it is highly detailed.

For all these modern kits there are some good upgrade and conversion sets, including some to fit out the interiors, from the aftermarket accessory makers. Some sets are made specifically to fit the Tamiya kits as well.

ABOVE **These T-34/85s in winter white are advancing toward Budapest in the winter of 1944/45. Apart from the new gun and larger turret there is little to distinguish them from late T-34/76s. The T-34/85 hull was almost completely unchanged apart from a sharp angle where the upper and lower glacis meet, an area where most T-34/76s had a rounded appearance.** *via Chris Ellis*

MODELLING THE T-34/76

T-34 MODEL 1942

I n the summer of 1941 the all-conquering German army turned its attentions to Russia, and in a lightning campaign reached the outskirts of Moscow, some 3,000km from its start lines, within four months. During this summer of victories the Germans were unpleasantly surprised by the power of the Russian tanks, particularly when they found themselves facing T-34s.

Although the Soviets did not initially distinguish themselves in their use of armour, as the campaign progressed they were able gradually to assimilate the tactics of the Germans. This critical fact, in conjunction with the mass production of tanks, was to be the key to eventual victory against the invader, and one of the crucial weapons in this victory was the T-34.

This chapter examines a T-34 Model 1942 manufactured in Krasnoye Sormovo Zadov No 112 (Gorki). It was characteristic of this plant to install PTK-5 periscopes into the turrets, as well as to add numerous handrails along the hull so that infantry could cling on to them. Another characteristic feature of this plant was to weld splash

BELOW **A side view of the completed model shows how its tracks should lie along the tops of the wheels. T-34 tracks were not a tight fit.**

guards — metal strips on the upper edge of the front and side panels around the turret ring — in order to divert enemy shells.

From close examination of contemporary photographs, the modeller identified three versions of the Model 1942, each differing in terms of their external fuel tanks. There were nine in the first production batch. The second had slab-sided containers on the rear mudguards, and the last was to have the typical cylindrical containers.

Other variations are also noticeable within each factory's annual output — the absence of a mantlet for the hull machine gun, the use of additional appliqué armour plating of over 35mm in the front of some units of the last type.

Assembly

The 1/35 scale Tamiya model is very old, but still quite good. It is easy to assemble and has a clean-cut, austere appearance. We need to begin by opening the ventilation grilles the length of the engine in order to put into position some excellent etched-brass accessories from On The Mark Models. This requires great attention to detail.

In order to assemble the Model 1942 version with rear fuel tanks, you will need to close up the holes for the defunct cylindrical tanks with

ABOVE **The splash guards which protected the turret ring are clearly seen in this view.**

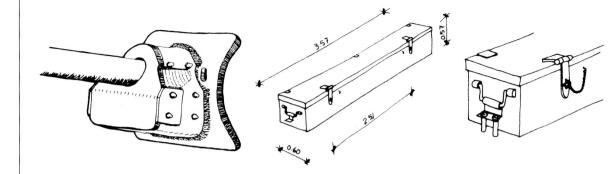

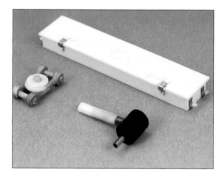

ABOVE LEFT **Detail of mantlet.**

ABOVE RIGHT **Crate measurements and lock detail. (See photo 14 page 48 for reference.)**

CENTRE RIGHT **Gun barrel and mantlet.**

CENTRE FAR RIGHT **The parts from On The Mark Models are complicated to assemble but the results are magnificent.**

BELOW RIGHT **Plastic has been used to recreate the tool crate. Other home-made improvements can also be appreciated.**

BELOW FAR RIGHT **Small hooks on the right side, made from copper wire.**

OPPOSITE, TOP **Hull showing modifications and additions.**

OPPOSITE, BOTTOM **The model nears completion following work on the turret and rear fuel tanks.**

putty, and then position the numerous handrails. This is easily done with thick copper wire from telephone cable. The small hooks for the straps which held additional track links can be made from finer copper wire.

The big join between the hull side and top panels isn't very good and needs a lot of work. It's necessary to fill in the hole with putty and simulate a line of solder by making small incisions in the putty.

We also had to add solder lines between various armoured panels, at the junction of the mudguards with the hull, and elements such as handrails or splash guards; these can be made from strips by Evergreen bevelled with a modelling knife.

Other parts to be added are the small catches next to the hooks for the towing cables. These can be made from small pieces of plastic, small pieces of tin and copper wire (see sketch on page 12).

The position of the headlamp needs to be changed and a tin bracket has to be made. Don't forget the headlamp electric cable which can be made from copper wire (see photo 15 on page 48 for a reference). You will also need to replace the machine gun with a hypodermic needle.

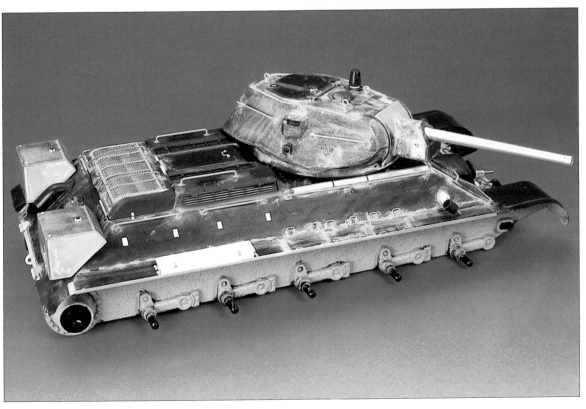

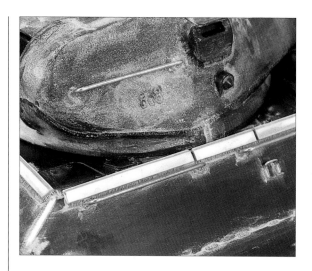

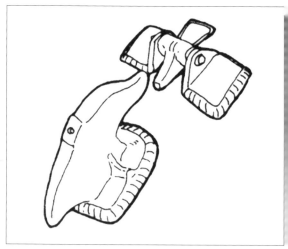

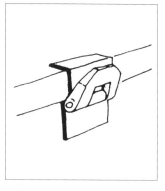

TOP LEFT **Turret detail. The weld lines have been made out of modelling putty and textured by small incisions made with a knife.**

TOP RIGHT **Hook for towing cable.**

ABOVE **Latch for small crate and side engine hatch.**

RIGHT **The two adjustable ventilation panels are made from fine aluminium sheeting, as are the fuel tanks.**

Two protective panels will need to be added to the area below the main ventilation grille of the engine. The part in the kit corresponding to the large removable rear panel fits poorly. You will need to cut off the ends of the mudguards and adjust this part using some strips of plastic imitating the edges of the steel panels and then replace the mudguards, adding rivets.

The crate holding cleaning materials that is provided in the kit is accurate, but a somewhat improved part can be made as shown in the accompanying photographs and diagrams (see page 10).

As far as the turret is concerned, apart from the handrails and armour soldering joints, you can also add serial numbers from any kit. The PTK-5 periscope is from a 1943 T-34 and the small hatchway hook can easily be made from scratch. The mantlet needs to be filed down on the left side, at an angle to allow for the gunner's line of vision, and the

lower section needs modifying as per the drawing (see page 10). Finally, the bevelling along the outer edge of the mudguards, as well as additional fuel tanks, needs to be created using strips of plastic, since those provided by the manufacturer are too small in scale.

Painting

For the base coat I mixed 60% Dark Green (XF-61), 10% Khaki and 20% Olive Green (XF-58) from Tamiya's acrylic range, adding shades of Dark Yellow (XF-60), Earth (SF-52) and Reddish Brown (XF-64), always using an airbrush.

I also applied various oil washes, increasing the variety of surfaces. To add the detail I used both airbrush and paintbrush, and finished off with gentle dry brushwork on protrusions to accentuate them.

ABOVE LEFT **The realistic effect of the ice cleats included in the Alhambra Models etched-metal set.**

ABOVE RIGHT **Spare track links are carried on the side of the turret.**

BELOW **The canvas roll can be made with dual component putty. Before assembling it we made copies for use in future models using a simple silicone mould.**

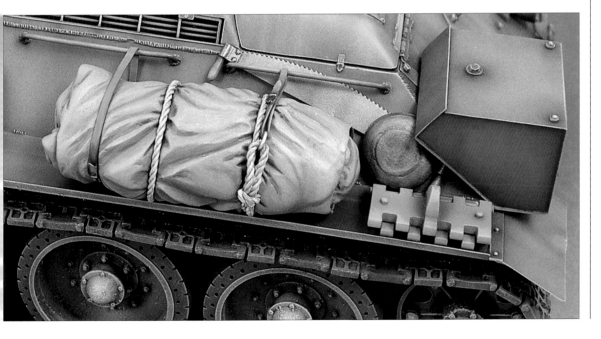

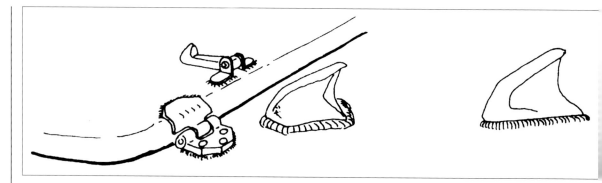

ABOVE **Hooks to hold the hatch open.**

RIGHT **Front view. Note the changed location of the headlamp. The periscope in the driver's hatch is from Alhambra Models.**

BELOW RIGHT **The box-shaped fuel tanks on the rear plate sit beside the exhaust pipes. Note the strut which supports each tank.**

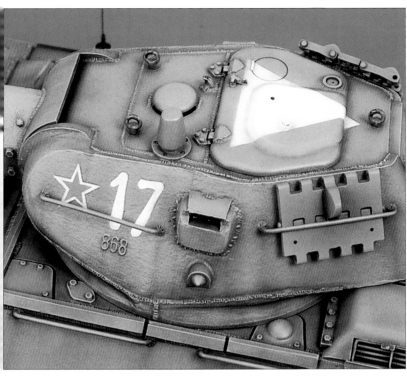

LEFT **The identification triangle, numbers and stars can be painted on by means of an airbrush and adhesive stencilling.**

BELOW **The completed engine deck grilles are much more realistic than the kit's plastic ones.**

MATERIALS USED

Tamiya T-34/76 Model 1942,
ref. 35049.

Alhambra Models etched-
metal, ref. 35-003 .

On The Mark Models etched-
metal, ref. TMP 3503.

Model Kasten tracks, ref K-5.

Jordi Rubio gun, ref. TG-07.

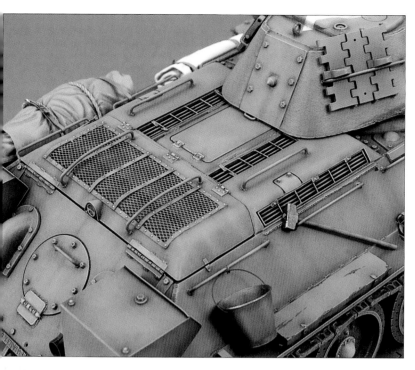

The finished article — the final finish is achieved with matt varnish by Marabu applied with an airbrush. This varnish has a reflective quality, which emphasises the volume.

T-34 STEP-BY-STEP

BELOW **The front-end mudguard of this Tamiya T-34 should be carefully cut using a small saw, removing by lightly pressing it off with your fingers. File down the surface to eliminate cut marks, and scrape the sides to make the piece thinner.**

OPPOSITE **In order to remove the mudguards from the Dragon model, use the scriber to make deep incisions, but break the piece manually. Once the sides are filed down, the new mudguards are fitted by gluing with cyanoacrylate.**

OPPOSITE, BOTTOM RIGHT **The texture found on the edge of the armoured surface and on the welding cords, can be rendered by lightly touching the plastic with the tip of a blade fixed to a wire, and attached to a small electric welder.**

The best T-34 chassis on the market is the one made by Dragon, corresponding to the T-34/85 Model 1944. To build an older T-34/76 model we can modify this chassis and use the turret, wheels and curved mudguards from either the Tamiya or Zvezda models. This section provides a step-by-step description of the assembly/transformation of one of these kits; many of the techniques and improvements outlined here can be effected on other kits.

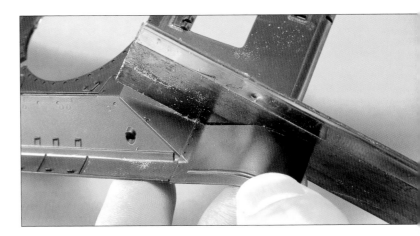

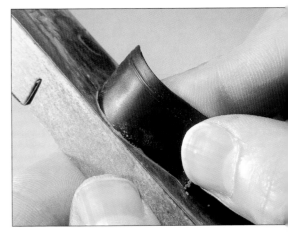

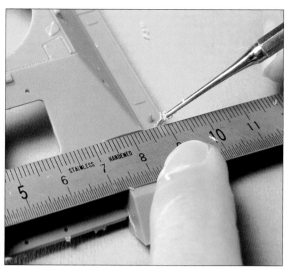

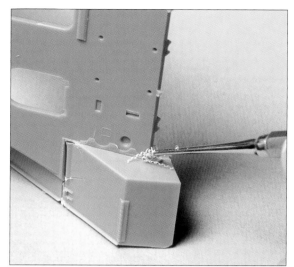

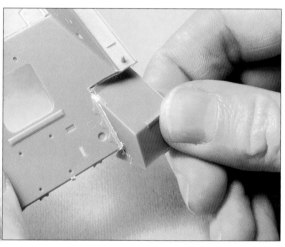

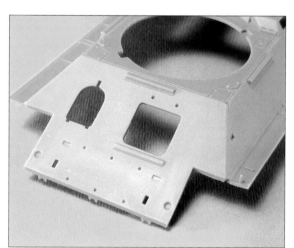

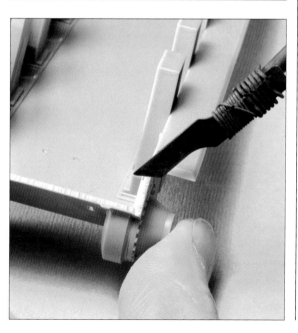

RIGHT **The small hooks on the hull sides should be removed with a knife blade.**

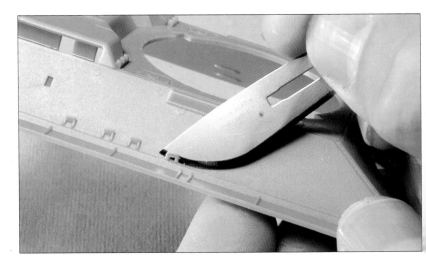

BELOW **Another place where weld marks need to be duplicated by lightly touching the plastic with the tip of a blade fixed to a wire, and attached to a small electric welder.**

BELOW RIGHT AND BOTTOM **The semicircular reinforcement piece found on the nose was made by carefully cutting and filing a 6.8mm plastic rod.**

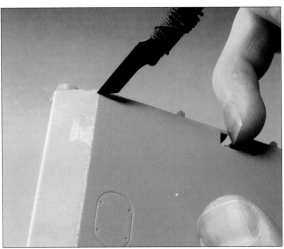

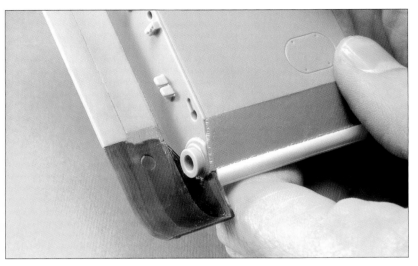

LEFT **The hull nose reinforcement is attached.**

BELOW LEFT **To imitate the mud found throughout the lower sections, apply a mixture of putty, fine sand, and nail-polish remover.**

BOTTOM LEFT **New mudguards and hull nose reinforcement in place.**

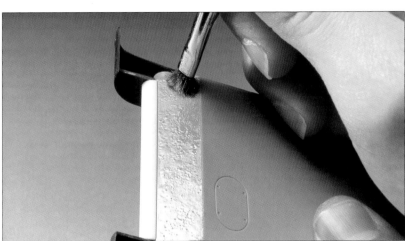

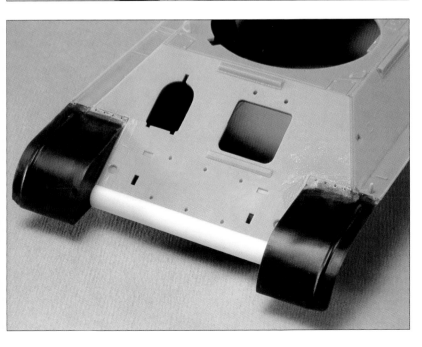

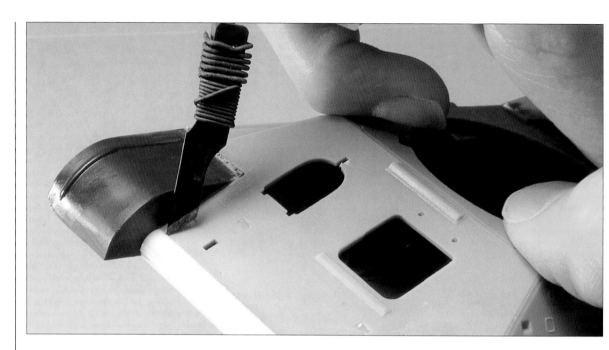

ABOVE AND RIGHT **After gluing the reinforcement to the hull front the weld marks were rendered using an electric 'hot knife'.**

OPPOSITE **The individual plastic track links can be joined using liquid cement and accurately lined up along a metal ruler. Once the cement begins to dry, fit the tracks onto the wheels. On the top run the track should sag slightly between the wheels — the result of the links' weight.**

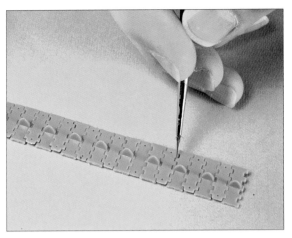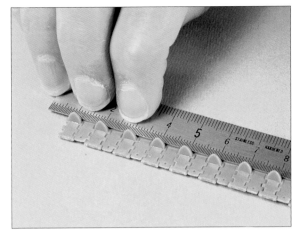

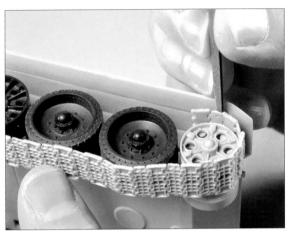

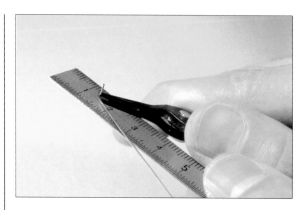

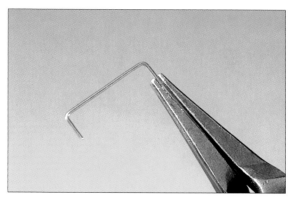

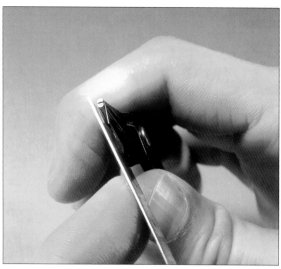

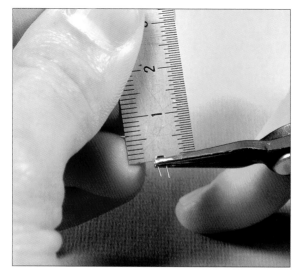

THIS PAGE **The hand rails were made using 0.6mm diameter galvanised wire, and flat-tip pliers to make the folds. The metallic hooks were made from 0.3mm copper thread, and a metallic ruler was applied to make the folds. The welding around these hooks and handles was rendered using the tip of a blade and putty.**

OPPOSITE **The metal vent of the engine, found on the top rear end of the vehicle, was hollowed out with the help of a small drill. A blade and finally a file, were used to complete the hollowing out of this part of the vehicle. Reinforcements were made using fine strips of plastic. Inside, cyanoacrylate was used to glue a piece of plastic netting cut to measure.**

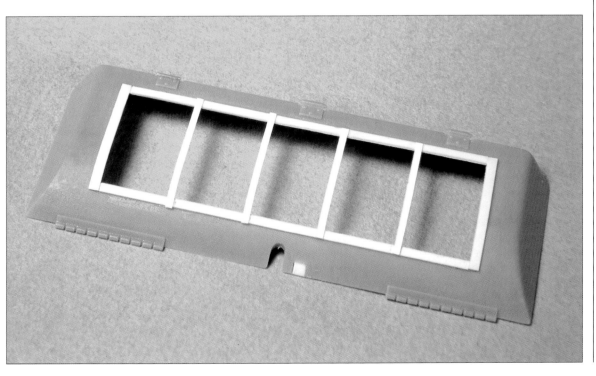

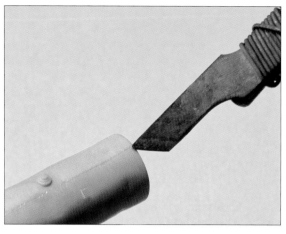

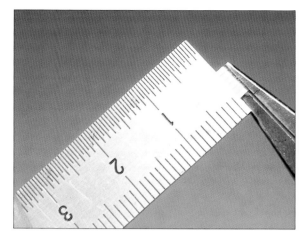

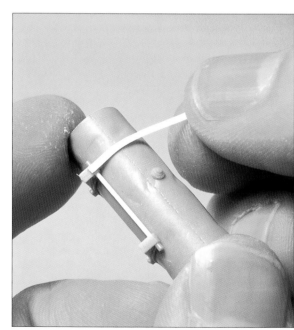

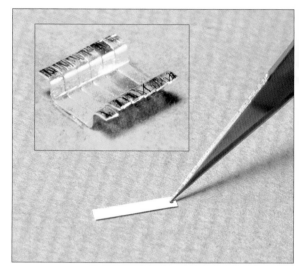

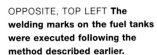

OPPOSITE, TOP LEFT **The welding marks on the fuel tanks were executed following the method described earlier.**

OPPOSITE, TOP RIGHT, OPPOSITE, CENTRE LEFT AND RIGHT **The fuel tank handles were made using brass strips from etched-metal kits. The strips were folded with pliers and a metallic ruler.**

OPPOSITE, BOTTOM LEFT **The six small hooks of the tanks were made from a fine strip of plastic.**

LEFT AND OPPOSITE, BOTTOM RIGHT **The tank retainers were made from an 0.13mm thick plastic sheet.**

BELOW LEFT AND BOTTOM LEFT **Two views of a finished drop tank.**

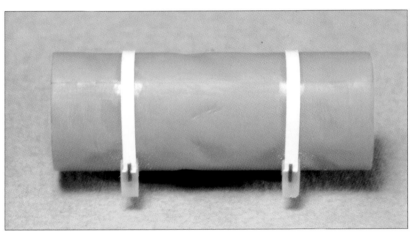

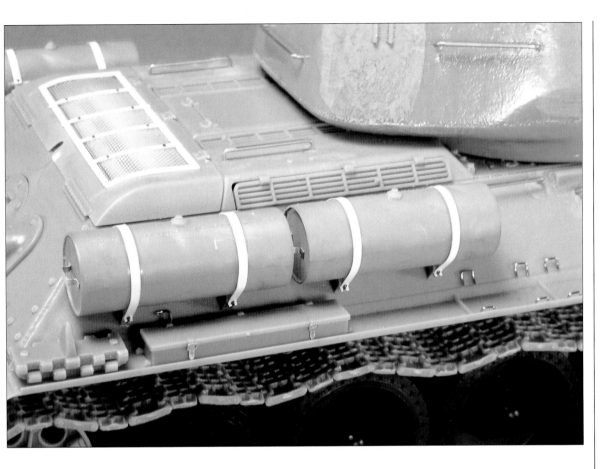

The drop tanks are positioned on the hull sides and the model is ready for painting.

RIGHT **Engine decking and exhaust detail.**

BELOW **Fine plastic sheets were used to render some of the front-end details; the periscope is a resin copy of a Tamiya Tiger piece.**

OPPOSITE, ABOVE LEFT AND RIGHT **The inside of the headlight was hollowed using a small ball-shaped router bit in a drill.**

OPPOSITE, BELOW **The headlight in position on the hull.**

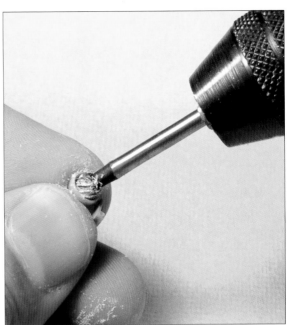

ABOVE **Knocked-out tanks were often used to shelter infantry positions.**

T-34/76 MODEL 1943

Sometime around 20 September 1942, the German Sixth Army reached the River Volga. The Soviet Fifty-second Army was isolated by Stalingrad docks and the river on a front some 25km long. The German Luftwaffe had transformed Stalingrad into a confused heap of rubble that hampered the movements of the advancing Panzers. In the epic street battles, the German offensive tactics — sweeping encirclements and Panzer thrusts — were ineffective, as the Russian General Chuikov tells us in his memoirs, 'The defenders of Stalingrad saw that combat tanks were coming within range of their guns and anti-tank weapons and, at the same time, that the German infantry was too far away from the tanks to provide protection, thereby transforming the enemy battle order.'

The bloodiest confrontations occurred in October during the German assault on the large industrial complexes of the city. Only a small sector of Stalingrad remained to be conquered, but on the opposite bank of the Volga the Russians had brought in the troops necessary to allow them — just — to sustain the defensive action. This trickle of reinforcements completely deceived the Germans who took

ABOVE **The only touch of colour on the tank is the air identification triangle painted on the turret roof.**

ABOVE LEFT **The rubble from demolished buildings has built up all around the tank.**

LEFT **Careful work on the rubble-strewn base gives the atmosphere of the Stalingrad fighting.**

them as proof of the shortage of Russian reserves. In reality, the Russians were tough Stalingrad survivors fighting on without reinforcements, who by this time were involved in a pitiless grinding struggle in which defence was easier than attack. The wastage of men and equipment was enormous and virtually unprecedented.

The Scene

This scene modelled faithfully depicts how the battle for Stalingrad was finally turned around. Tanks were almost immobile and rendered virtually useless by the piles of ruined buildings blocking the streets. Stalingrad was a remorselessly bloody urban battle where literally every house was a position to be defended. The burden of the battle, therefore, fell on the infantry units, which often got involved in hard man-to-man fighting, to win small patches of land.

Here we see a group of German soldiers using a 80mm mortar beside a T-34 abandoned by its crew. The scene matches a series of photographs taken during the battle of Stalingrad. For our scene we decided to take advantage of the figures included in the new Tamiya German Infantry Mortar Team kit, which are in full action poses and consequently add great drama to the scene.

33

T-34/76 Model 1943

Although this version of the T-34 is known as the 1943 model, it actually entered service at the end of 1942, just in time to go into action during the battle of Stalingrad. We used a Tamiya kit to which we added an etched-brass set from Eduard and tracks from Model Kasten, as well as some home-made pieces. We made the cover of the external chest from aluminium sheet, which was also used for the turret interior, which was completed with home made parts.

The painting of the model itself was the most interesting and enjoyable part owing to the attractive effects of dirt and damage shown by the tank in the original photograph. The dust accumulated over the whole surface is the most obvious detail, so dense in some areas that it even obscures the basic colour. We made up this colour using Tamiya acrylics mixing the following: Sky (XF-21), Light Blue (XF-23), Bright Green (XF-26), Olive Green (XF-58), Dark Green (XF-61) and Olive Drab (XF-62).

The ageing process was simulated by covering the tank with a wash of black oil paint. Next, we began the dust covering and discolouration of the base colour, for which we made up a series of oil colour washes, heavily thinned with turpentine. First, we made a general wash, darkening it as it approached those areas where the dust was greatest. For this we started with yellow ochre oil paint, then added a little contrast with natural sienna oil which is somewhat darker. Finally, we finished off this effect with a last wash prepared with a combination of Humbrol enamels: Matt White (34), Cream (71) and Desert Yellow (93). The final touches were applied with a subtle wash of white oil applied to certain areas only, trying to avoid an excessively uniform appearance. Then one could apply a light film with an airbrush using a mixture of Tamiya acrylics thinned with water, in our case, White (XF-2) and Buff (XF-57). This mixture was applied to the wheels and lower parts of the vehicle, but not too brightly.

The white triangle on the top of the turret is an aerial identification mark which was made by masking and airbrushing. The accumulated earth in the skirts was obtained with dry tea leaves and earth mixed with agua-plast.

The tank tracks were painted graphite grey with a mixture of Black (XF-1) and Grey Blue (XF-66) and had a second and last wash with the same colour.

The interior of the turret was painted white, which was later made to look dirty with washes of black and dark green oils. The streaks were made with grey graphite mixed from Vallejo acrylic colours.

The tow cable was made by using the cable heads from the kit and some scale 'rope' as sold for model shipbuilding. It was painted dark brown and given a rusty finish with orange brown.

On the unditching log (which was the one from the kit) I added texture with a modelling saw. This was scraped along the log so that its teeth cut grooves like the grain of a piece of wood. Afterwards I painted it with Earth (XF-52) and a wash of black oil paint, followed by dry-brushing with white (Humbrol 34) and Desert Yellow (Humbrol 63).

The headlamp was hollowed out and a piece of aluminium cooking foil placed inside as a reflector. The strap hanging on the right side was also made from aluminium foil.

The ground was painted once it had thoroughly dried. For this we used Buff (XF-57), which we lightened with a little white. Take care not to paint more of the parts than is necessary. To give the whole thing a more realistic note, some of the rubble was painted as if it were pieces of tile or flagstone. Finally, washes of yellow ochre and natural sienna were applied, the first a general one and the second concentrating on

the shade and sunken ground areas to add the impression of mass to the ground. The final touches in the darkest and most sunken areas were finished with Dark Earth. The rods and rusty tubing were painted with Humbrol Skin Colour (62) to which, while wet, I selectively applied a black oil wash.

The mantle and the hatch, which had been thrown to the ground by the force of the explosion that destroyed the tank, were made with two-part epoxy putty.

The abandoned GAZ-67B machine gun came from the Tamiya kit . The machine gun was painted with a mixture of Vallejo Military Green (975) and Dark Grey (994). Afterwards, I applied a wash of black oil and, when this was dry, I applied patches of a lighter colour made with a mixture of Vallejo Military Green, Light Grey (990) and Chocolate Brown (872). Some touches of aluminium colour were added in the darkest areas and on the edges.

ABOVE **Dirt thrown up by shell and bomb explosions does not settle uniformly. It builds up in particular around the edges of raised parts like the driver's periscopes and the hull machine gun, as shown here.**

LEFT **The wood grain effect on the log must be carefully painted if it is to look realistic.**

MODELLING THE T-34/85

This scene is based on one of the hundreds of photos taken of abandoned Soviet equipment as. It depicts a Russian T-34/85 tank with a broken track which, once immobilised, was easily captured by German troops as they progressed across the Russian Steppes. The T-34/76 Tamiya model (ref. 35049) was the base for the tank, which was improved by adding Eduard and Verlinden etched-brass kits, the MB T-34/85 D-5T resin turret, together with the Jordio Rubio gun (ref. TG-09) plus a few extra details.

MATERIALS USED

Tamiya T-34/76 Model 1942, ref. 35049.

Eduard etched-brass kit, ref. 35069.

Verlinden etched-brass kit, ref. 968.

MB T-34/85 D-5T resin turret

Model Kasten tracks, ref K-5.

Jordi Rubio gun, ref. TG-09.

RIGHT **A broken track will trail like this behind a tank which was moving forward at the time it was hit. The damage to the thin metal track guard was reproduced with a mini-drill fitted with a grinding wheel or milling cutter. The plastic was ground away from under the track guard until the desired effect was achieved.**

The front mudguard looks as if has been damaged — this was done by applying gentle heat with a soldering iron, taking great care not to bring it so near the plastic that it melted. On the burned rear end the slender bodywork was exposed, corroded by heat and oxidation; this was achieved by working on it with a mini-drill and grinding wheel to wear away the inside. To make the four rubber wheels appear burnt, I filed almost all the rubber away to leave only the internal cavity. Some brass hoops were added to each wheel to simulate the structure of the rubber. The broken track is by Model Kasten (ref. K-5), the other from the Tamiya kit.

Painting

The tank was painted in the basic Tamiya acrylic colour (XF-27). After painting the slogans on each side of the turret with 75% Vallejo A-92 acrylics, I applied a wash over the whole tank. Once this wash was dry, I applied very fine brush strokes with Vallejo B-89, but only on the front part of the tank, since the rear would be in a different colour. Finally, I applied some streaks of dirt, rust, patches of flaking paint, etc.

ABOVE **Letters and numerals on the turret, applied with a paint brush.**

BELOW **The effect of dirt and dust on the front of the body.**

BOTTOM **The broken left track sags between the wheels due to its weight. Model Kasten separate track links allow this effect to be created.**

ABOVE **The broken track and burnt wheels are completed by the piles of ash from the burnt rubber tyres.**

The burnt area was outlined by airbrushing a black stain over the width of the tank to show the scorch marks resulting from the burning tank with all its many types of material. The burnt effect was continued with a range of colours such as oranges, browns, yellows, reds and black, depending on the material affected. All these colours were applied with a flat brush to pick out the various textures on the surface, creating a range of irregular colours. Then all the joints in the bodywork — bolts, handles, etc. — were painted with dilute black. When all this was dry, using a thin brush, I painted the dark brown and black stains with snake-shaped streaks. Using torn up newspaper, I camouflaged some parts of the surface by giving it small touches of pastel chalk colour in dark blood red and ochre on some of the burnt areas.

The Ground

For the base I used a piece of extruded polystyrene, to which I applied a fine layer of Agua-plast mixture with added white sand and adhesive. Before this mixture dried, I imprinted some wheel marks of different types and dimension as well as soldiers' footprints and horses' hoof marks.

The tank itself was fixed to the base and I had to adjust the ground to the tank tracks so that there was no gap between the two. I did this by preshaping then applying Milliput. Additionally I simulated the sand displaced by the weight of the tank.

The base ground was divided into two parts — the road and the vegetation. The entire surface was initially painted the same, with various colours of sand, ochres, greys, browns, etc. These were applied in the same way as I painted the burnt surface of the tank. When all this was completely dry, I used a dry brush to paint the track area an off-white colour to make all the footprints and track marks stand out. On part of the grassed area I then applied a mixture of white adhesive and water — the consistency of milk — and at the same time I laid Verlinden Static Lawn (ref. 638), giving it various light touches with a dry brush.

The burnt rubber ash from the wheels was simulated by modelling Milliput into small irregular-sized piles painted different shades of grey. When these were dry, I applied a coat of white adhesive mixed with water to the piles and tops of the wheel cavities. While this was still wet, I dropped cigarette ash over the adhesive.

Final Touches

The front of the tank was dusted with Humbrol Khaki Drill colour; simultaneously I painted the tracks with the same colour, afterwards giving them a touch of Humbrol silver using a dry brush. The burnt areas of the ground were airbrushed black in different ways to give a varied effect. After the black paint had dried on the road I dry-brushed the patches with khaki and grey colour and painted the grassy areas as if there were fire tracks, matching them afterwards with some ochre, green and white.

Finally, the figure in the scene is a Verlinden soldier with a Hornet jacket and some added uniform details.

ABOVE LEFT **The burnt area of the turret. All the colours were applied with a brush, over an airbrushed base of black.**

ABOVE **The burnt rubber on the wheels, converted to ash, is modelled with two-part putty.**

BELOW **To reproduce the burnt parts, a varied range of colours was used.**

T-34/85 MODEL 1944

OPPOSITE, TOP **Remains of leaves and fallen branches across the entire surface, made out of thyme and oregano.**

OPPOSITE, BOTTOM **The absence of sections of the mudguards was very common on T-34 tanks.**

OPPOSITE, CENTRE **Rear view with mudguards broken and missing, and an accumulation of mud.**

BELOW **The Tamiya T-34/85 builds into a very convincing model.**

The Tamiya T-34 requires a lot of scratch-built detailing, mainly consisting of the addition or substitution of plastic pieces by brass or metal wire — in particular the grab handles and latches that feature on the turret and the hull. The best way of identifying these details, is to consult photographs and plans in the specialist publications identified in the Bibliography on page 62. The largest job is the elimination of the plastic engine grille and its replacement by a metal grille of the correct size. Another significant job involves the representation of thick, coarse welding around almost the full circumference of the turret. This is made from little balls of putty put in place using a brush moistened in pure acetone and moulded using a modelling knife.

Painting

An airbrush, a dry brush and washes were used. First, the airbrush was used to apply the base coat and to highlight and volumise: shading in hollows and thinning down flat areas. As the T-34 is painted in a single colour, the variations are important to show wear and tear, corrosion,

ageing and all the other things that lead to discolouration of the paintwork.

After the base coats were applied by airbrush, the dry brush was used to make ridges and other details stand out. Finally, using washes of dark colours, I outlined individual rivets, screws, handles, hatches and so on to help all the details to stand out. In addition, washes are a highly suitable way to paint the muddy areas of the tank, grease marks, areas where there is rust and so on.

This tank is basically painted dark green, a colour that is often represented badly in publications, with no two looking the same. In this case it is also difficult to be precise about the amount of each colour applied, since there was a lot of ad hoc mixing of several colours by eye and then much work went into the representation of wear and tear. The foliage added to the surface of the tank give it a touch of personality. They are made out of stalks and dry leaves obtained from florists' shops, stuck on with white glue mixed with water, painted a green colour using an airbrush and then retouched in various shades of green and some yellow.

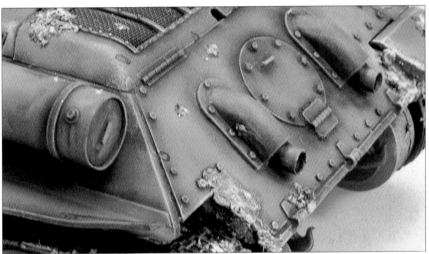

RIGHT **Side view showing details of camouflage and markings.**

BELOW RIGHT **The hooks on the rear part of the turret are made from wire. The engine grille is made from very fine wire mesh. The ring of welding marks next to the rear hooks indicates frequent use.**

BOTTOM RIGHT **The tow cables are attached to the hooks ready for instant use.**

OPPOSITE **General views of the vehicle in which the general wear and tear to the paintwork can be appreciated.**

T-34/85 CROATIA

During the Balkan Civil War the various opposing factions found the need to distinguish exactly who controlled the many captured vehicles. They did this by means of very conspicuous camouflage of a type which is useless in the majority of conflicts. Furthermore, in many cases they painted slogans on the vehicles proclaiming the insignia of their countries or leaders. This allows us a chance to produce an interesting diorama using a T-34/85.

We took as the reference material for our T-34 model the various photographs in the Concord book *The Balkans on Fire* which shows a number of T-34s modified by Croatian soldiers after being captured from the Serbs.

The T-34, although obsolete in this war, served mainly as mobile artillery and its participation was hardly momentous. But in the modeller's eyes it is an attractive vehicle because of its unusual modifications. For example, it was fitted with modern wheels from the Russian T-55 and with headlamps from the same tank. But the most

surprising change is the amateurish location of a Browning 0.5-inch M2HB machine gun on the rear section of the turret, which was supplied from American or Russian ammunition boxes as carried by the Dushkas. At first sight this seems incongruous, but it is logical when you realise that the former Yugoslavian army used both Eastern and Western armaments.

Another important difference is the change in the basic T–34 colour from the original Soviet (very dark) green. The Yugoslavs painted their tanks in a much brighter green in common with the rest of the Yugoslavian fleet. Over this green were painted the regulation numbers in white.

When captured by the Croats, the most peculiar phase started — with a huge assortment of colours from sprays and cans of paint, the soldiers camouflaged the whole tank with no attempt at an organised scheme, the only limitation being the number of colours available. The order and shapes were entirely random. The artists also left areas unpainted, either because they ran out of paint or because they did not consider it important. In our model, the rear section was not camouflaged — nor was the front of the gun.

Although the soldiers used non-military colours, so to speak, it is important to interpret the paint job to scale, since in reality the colours were so vivid they were quickly affected by bad weather as well as vehicle use and abuse. Our particular protagonist used a peculiar camouflage of two colour streamers: a red lead as used for priming metal parts, and a yellow. To make these markings, we selected a suitable size brush to get the spray to scale.

The slogans around the tank were done by hand with a paint brush using a variety of different colours. It rather goes against the grain to paint the tank with these strange colours and even gets unpleasant when painting those horrible letters all over the bodywork! But it had to be done to give the correct 'feel' to the model. Finally, it must be stressed that the lower parts of the majority of the tanks were not normally painted.

Funnily enough, making the model dirty was perhaps the hardest task, since we didn't want to add any more colour. In this case a very dirty whitish mud found in the Dubrovnik area was chosen. Remember that mud is found in a variety of colours, from greys to reds or black depending on the soil colour local to the area. This mud, converted into dust by the heat of the sun, gets into every crevice of the tank, giving it a whitish cast; but because of the movement and activities of the crew there are some cleaner and more burnished areas.

We are not giving colour references because there are so many different paints and camouflages that it would take too long to name each one. Literally almost any colour can be used for vehicles taking part in this conflict; what is much more important are the concepts and conclusions already explained.

The streaks are also fundamental to the finished job — even if this is only a pair of oxide and dark green streaks belonging to the original Russian green. Finally, when all the detail painting is finished, the last job is to apply all the typical wear and tear effects of each tank — such as spilt oil, leaking water, mud splashes, corroded metal etc.

OPPOSITE, TOP LEFT **The effects of dried mud are applied all over the tank, giving it a whitish appearance. But it is the other markings that make this vehicle so distinctive. It was usual for a crew to personalise their tank with its own name.**

The Slovenes, for example, painted on most of their captured vehicles the sign TO, *Teritorialna Obramada* **(Territorial Army) in white. The Croats put the letters ZNG (JNA) on their vehicles and the Bosnians BiH (Bosnia and Herzegovina).**

Not all slogans were political, sometimes the soldiers wrote the names of their loved ones or their home towns and some vehicles even appeared with more modern names such as 'U2', 'Bomb' or 'Alf'.

What they did have in common, however, was their extremely poor calligraphy and the use of bright contrasting colours such as yellow, ultramarine or vermilion.

The point therefore, is use your own freehand to paint the wording rather than use the usual masks or transfers, and make sure that it is irregular and blurred into the bargain.

OPPOSITE, CENTRE **The wheels of this T-34/85 belong to a T-55 tank.**

OPPOSITE, BOTTOM **An original detail is the Browning machine gun mounted on the turret.**

WALKROUND

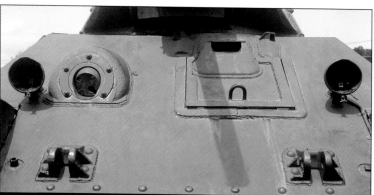

1 The main grille of the engine deck was not very strong and often showed dents in its mesh and bends in its framework. This example has had bars added by museum staff to prevent further damage.

2 Early T-34/76s had a pistol port in their turret rears. The port's plug is shown here.

4 The glacis of a T-34/76 Model 1941 shows all the early features — two headlamps instead of one, early driver's hatch with a single fixed periscope, hull machine gun mount without an external mantlet and early tow points.

5 This type of gun recoil housing was used on most T-34/76s after the Model 1940 which used a rounded casting.

7 Some T-34/76s carried a stowage bin on their hull side. Note that there's a gap between it and the hull plate.

8 The earliest T-34/76s had an oblong hatch in their rear plates for access to the transmission. The round hatch seen here soon replaced it and remained the standard type until the end of T-34/85 production.

3 This is the main style of early T-34 track, which used two different types of link.

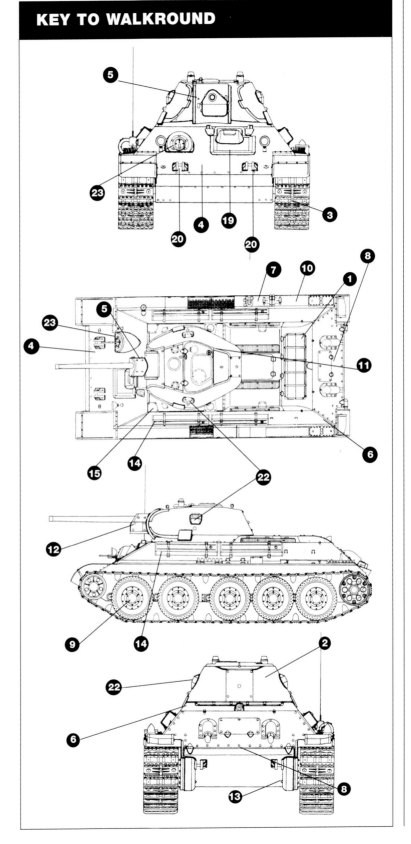

6 Here you can see how the hull's rear plate is fixed with the sideplate overlapping it.

9 This is the very common 'dished' road wheel with a perforated rubber tyre.

10 Many T-34s carried fuel drums on their sides. This top view shows how their securing straps were attached.

11 A closeup of the ventilator covers on a T-34/85 Model 1944 turret.

14 Tool boxes were attached to the trackguards like this.

15 Headlamp wiring is easily added to a model.

16 The inside of the commander's hatch of a T-34/85.

19 The inside of the driver's hatch shows details of his periscope mount.

20 This is the common style of tow hook, quite different to the early type shown in photo 4. The weld marks above it show where a securing clip was mounted.

21 This is the inside of the loader's hatch of a T-34/85.

12 This is the T-34/85 gun mantlet used from the Model 1944 to the end of production.

13 A close-up of the final drive armoured housing at the hull rear.

17 Many T-34s carried a two-man saw in this V-shaped bracket on the hull side.

18 Some T-34s carried drum-shaped smoke canisters at the rear. This is a top view showing how they were attached — a different fitting to the fuel drums seen in photo 10.

22 The cast side view port of a T-34/76 turret.

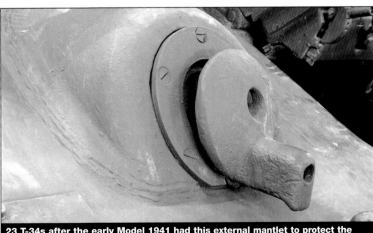

23 T-34s after the early Model 1941 had this external mantlet to protect the hull machine gun.

SCALE DRAWINGS

T-34/76 Model 1941

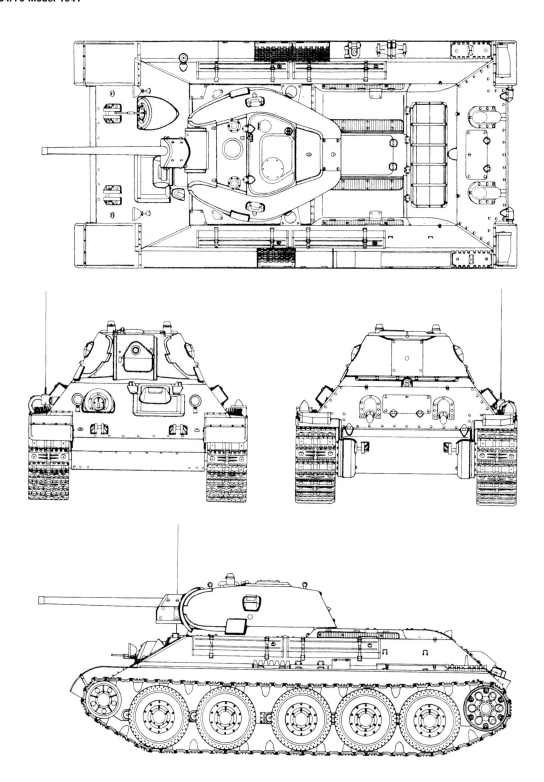

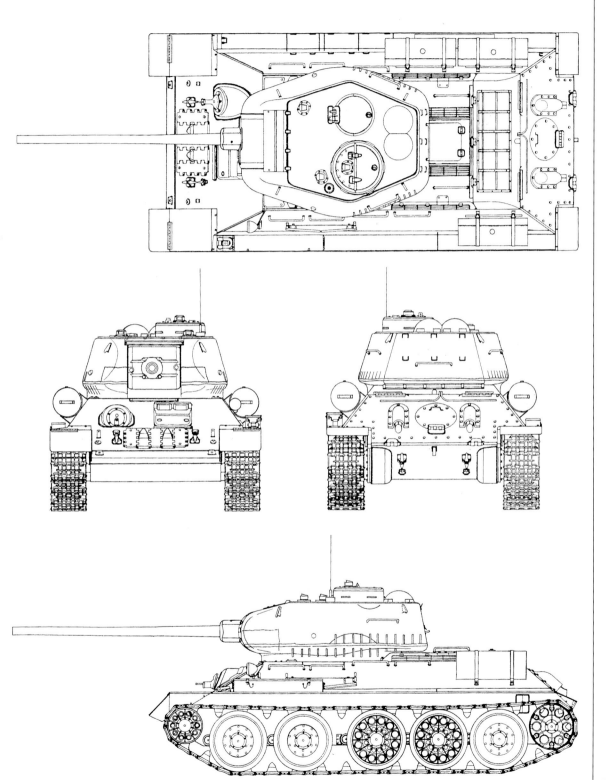

T-34/76 Variants

THIS PAGE (FROM TOP TO BOTTOM)
1 Model 1940 with cast turret, KLPX 1941 production.
2 Model 1941–42 with welded turret, STZ 1942 production.
3 Model 1942 with cast turret manufactured at Krasnoye Sormovo Zadov No 112 (Gorki).

OPPOSITE PAGE (FROM TOP TO BOTTOM)
4 Model 1941–42 with cast turret, STZ 1942 production.
5 Model 1943 with laminate turret, autumn 1943 production.
6 Model 1943 ChTZ autumn 1942 production.
7 Model 1943 with soft edge turret and cupola.

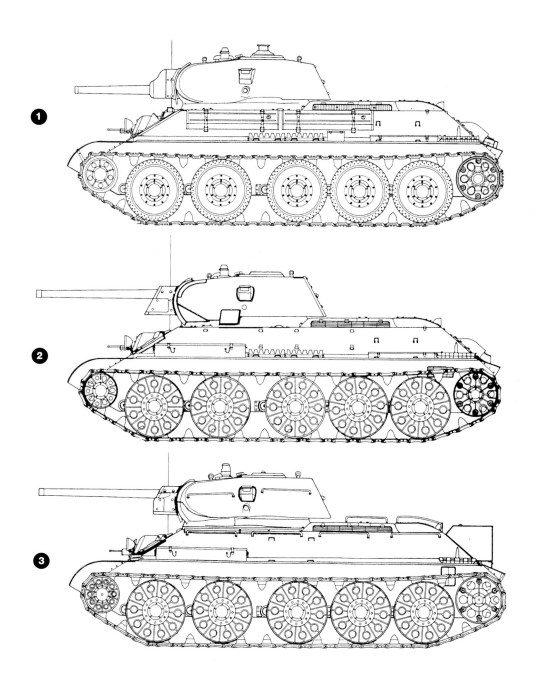

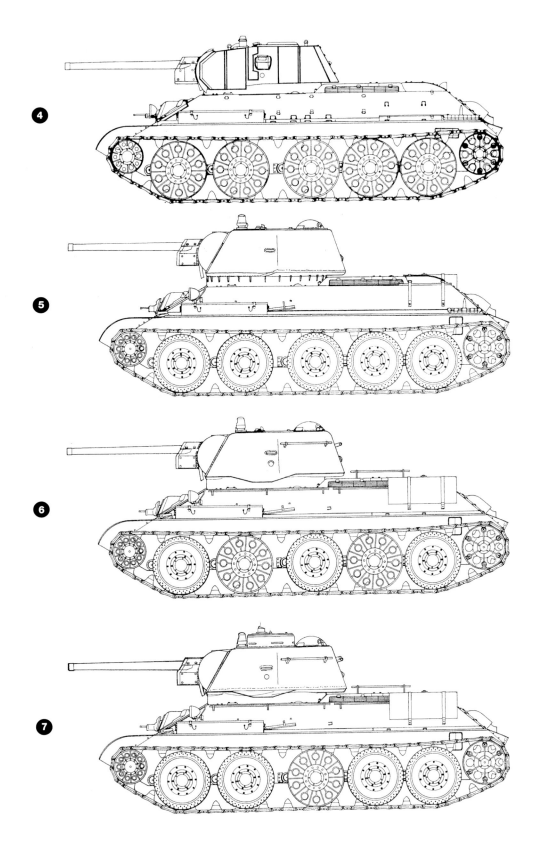

4

5

6

7

CAMOUFLAGE AND MARKINGS

CAMOUFLAGE COLOURS AND PATTERNS

It is often thought that all World War II Soviet tanks were simply painted dark green, but this is far from the truth. Apart from the obvious white winter overpainting, there were also many other variations.

Looking at that basic green first, the standard colour is usually identified as equivalent to the US FS595 reference colour 34102. This won't mean much unless you have that book of colour standards, but fortunately several model paint manufacturers label their tins or bottles with the FS595 equivalent. The most easily available paint range in the UK is Humbrol, which is not so labelled, but that company's 117, US Light Green, is the correct shade. According to Humbrol's own colour chart matching paints in other ranges are Testor's 1713 and Gunze Sangyo Mr Color 303. David H Klaus' IPMS Color Cross-Reference Guide gives Gunze Sangyo H330, Modelmaster 1713 and Floquil M199 as further equivalents but there does not yet appear to be a suitable match in the widely distributed Tamiya range. Remember that wartime Soviet paint production was not necessarily high quality or matched exactly to a colour standard in the first place, and that paint colours can change and fade when exposed to the weather over time. Although the suggested paints may not match each other exactly, all should be within the range of colours which the original paint could show. The combat life of most T-34s was quite short, so the paint would not have faded much if at all before the tank was either knocked out or returned to the

RIGHT **Ersatz camouflage from the Bosnian conflict. See pages 44–45.**

CAMOUFLAGE COLOURS AND PATTERNS

Careful application of weathering effects adds greatly to the realism of a model.

Remember camouflage is not necessarily the final coat of paint on a model: this has washes to simulate the effects of weathering and damage.

Glacis of Tamiya's T-34/76 Model 1942 showing typical winter whitewash camouflage.

Typical Russian dark green camouflage with overpainted white tactical marking and Soviet star.

factory for major repair — which would have included repainting in the official colour.

In winter a white overpainting was often applied. This could be a fairly solid coat, and there is some evidence that tanks produced in winter were painted white at the factory. More roughly applied white finishes were more common, and some T-34/76s showed an interesting scheme of white bands over the basic green with a 'mesh' pattern in white on the exposed green.

Going beyond the plain green or white colour schemes, some Soviet tanks carried two or three-colour camouflage with earth brown and/or sand patches or bands added to the green. Blotched or dappled schemes, like those often applied to German tanks, do not seem to have been used. No colour matches to paint ranges are at present available, but the brown seems to have been quite dark and the sand fairly tan in shade. The references quoted later show examples of these.

There is also a persistent story that T-34s produced at the Stalingrad factory during the German siege of that city were sometimes driven off the production lines and straight into action without their green paint. Anyone thinking of modelling this should bear in mind that the Stalingrad T-34s had several distinguishing features which will need to be reproduced as discussed in the modelling section and that a shiny bare steel appearance is the last thing to be expected. It seems most likely that any unpainted T-34s lacked only their green final coat, leaving a red-brown primer exposed. Alternatively they may have been unprimed, in which case the rust which formed on the steel would be visible. This would be basically red-brown too, but perhaps more

BELOW **Russian basic green camouflage seen on a Tamiya T-34/85.**

variable between orangey new rust and fairly dark brown old rust according to how long previously the individual hull, turret and other parts had been made.

Post-war T-34/85 production and use was by several Warsaw pact countries as well as the USSR, and the Polish, Czech and German basic greens were lighter than the Soviet one. Humbrol 120, Light Green, seems a reasonable match for these. T-34/85s were also exported to many client states in the Middle East, Africa, North Korea and North Vietnam. Middle Eastern T-34s were delivered in their manufacturer's green and usually overpainted with the local version of sand paint, which often wore off in places showing the green beneath, but those sold to Africa, Vietnam and Korea remained in their original green.

MARKINGS

Although the red star is assumed by many to be the quintessential Soviet marking it was very rarely seen on wartime tanks. Many T-34s carried only a tactical number on their turret sides. Much remains unknown about these, but it does seem that most units numbered in sequence with either three or four-digit codes. The numbers seem to have been hand-painted, often fairly crudely, at least as often as being applied with neat stencils, and the Cyrillic style of numbers was used rather than the 'Latin' style used by the Germans and the Western Allies. Examples can be found in the books suggested in the reference section.

Patriotic slogans were popular, 'For the Motherland' and 'For Stalin' often being seen. Presentation markings such as 'Dmitri Donskoi' appeared on tanks which had been paid for by public subscription in a particular area, by an organisation such as the Orthodox church, or even by an individual. How any individual in a communist society became rich enough to buy a tank is not recorded!

Air identification markings to prevent friendly air attack were carried on some tanks in 1941–42 but became much more common from late 1944 onwards, when the Soviet army came within range of Western air forces and a way had to be found to prevent them from being attacked by mistake. A white triangle on the turret top was the first marking introduced, but was replaced by a large white cross covering the whole turret top and often accompanied by a white band around the turret sides and rear.

The final form of markings found on Soviet T-34s is the unit symbol. These were usually geometric, such as various forms of circle or triangle which might have single, double or even triple lines. Others were more abstract, such as erect 'tombstone' shapes with discs inside their rounded tops or horizontal lines with squares attached under them. Some units used arrow shapes and others the shapes of animals or birds. Most have still not been attributed to a particular unit but some are known and can be found in the reference sources listed later.

Warsaw Pact and other non-Middle Eastern client state markings varied from the Polish red-and-white square (a Polish eagle was carried before this) and the Czech red, white and blue segmented roundel to small versions of national flags and variations on the red star marking. Middle Eastern T-34s tended to have no markings beyond a turret number or a patriotic slogan.

ABOVE **Typical examples of tactical numbers, unit markings and slogans.**

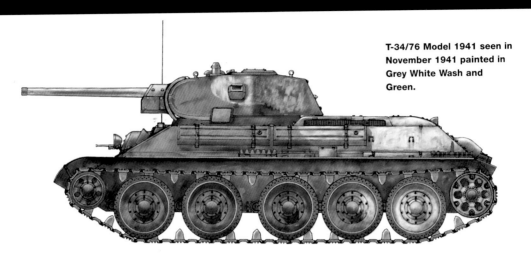

T-34/76 Model 1941 seen in
November 1941 painted in
Grey White Wash and
Green.

T-34/76 Model 1941–42
seen on the Leningrad Front
in autumn 1942. It is
painted in Olive Green 3b
and Earth Brown.

T-34/76 Model 1943 of the
251st Independent Tank
Regiment seen in January
1944. It has whitewash over
Olive Green 3b.

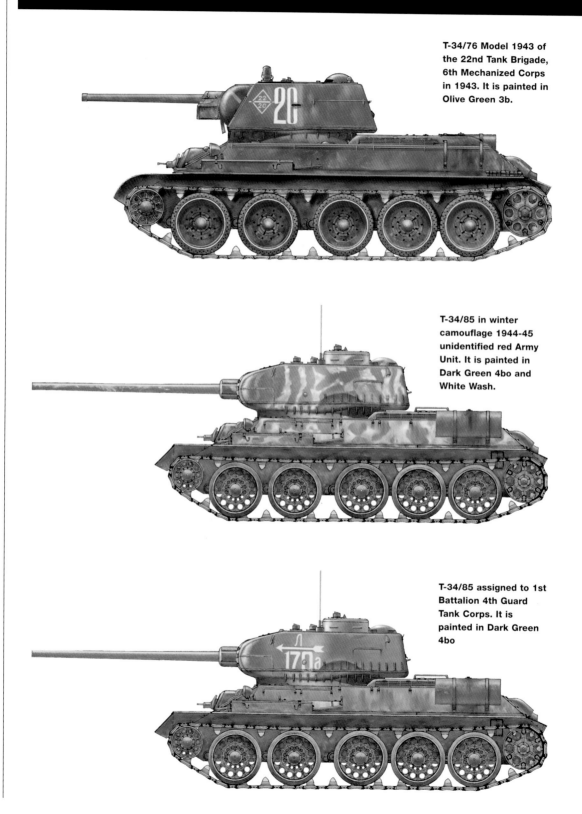

T-34/76 Model 1943 of the 22nd Tank Brigade, 6th Mechanized Corps in 1943. It is painted in Olive Green 3b.

T-34/85 in winter camouflage 1944-45 unidentified red Army Unit. It is painted in Dark Green 4bo and White Wash.

T-34/85 assigned to 1st Battalion 4th Guard Tank Corps. It is painted in Dark Green 4bo

MODEL ROUNDUP

T-34 kits are available in various scales, as already mentioned in the introduction where comments on them are given. To go with these full kits there are also quite few accessories, upgrades and conversions. The following lists give those that are were available at the time of writing, although some need to be hunted for and there is not enough space to give full listings for some accessory and conversion makers. Unlike the kits, accessory and upgrade sets can be hard to find. Study the advertisements in the model magazines published in your country for stockists outside the UK.

Aber has produced four etched-metal sets for T-34 models. Two cover details of the T-34/85, another gives track guards to replace the plastic ones of any kit, and the fourth builds the cylindrical fuel tank carried on the tank's sides and the smoke canisters sometimes carried on the rear plate. Rating *** B. The UK agent is Historex Agents, telephone 01304 206720, Email *Sales@historex-agents.demon.co.uk.*

Anvil Productions of Australia has three aftermarket track sets for any T-34 kit, giving all three of the main track types. These are resin, with excellent detail. They need very little cleaning up to be ready to use, and they simply snap together which makes them the easiest type of track to use for a model. Rating *** A. They are not yet available outside Australia, but Anvil can be reached at Anvil Miniatures, P.O. Box 538, Mayfield, NSW 2304, Australia or Email *anviljb@mpx.com.au.* Credit cards are taken and the sets are well worth the effort to get them.

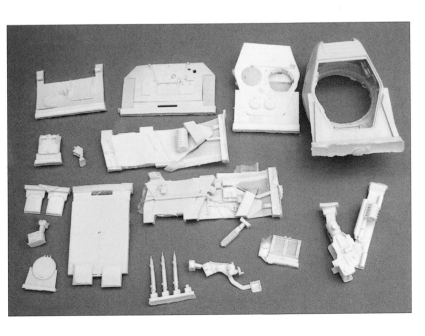

LEFT **Jaguar of the US makes a very nice T-34 interior set. Here are the main parts together with a few of the smaller details. Jaguar also has a T-34 engine set.**

ABOVE **Tamiya's T-34/76 kits were produced many years ago but still resurface from time to time. This is their original kit of the Model 1942 with a cast turret.**

KITS *(all polystyrene except where indicated)*

MAKER   VARIANT   **RATING**
1/76 & 1/72 scale

Matchbox/Revell
        T-34/76 Model 1942
        (*now available from Revell*)   ** A
Esci T-34/76 Model 1943   ** A
Fujimi T-34/76 Model 1942   *** A
        T-34/85 Model 1945   *** A
The Esci and Fujimi kits appear to be out of production but can still be found in model shops

Airfix T-34/85   * A
1/48

Bandai T-34/76
1/35
(*two kits, both with some interior detail*)   ** A

Dragon T-45/85 Model 1944   *** A
        T-34/85 Model 1945   *** A

Italeri T-34/76 Model 1943   *** B
        T-34/85 Model 1944   *** B

RPM/Maquette
        T-34/85 Model 1945   *** B

Tamiya T-34/76 Model 1942   ** A
        T-34/76 Model 1943   ** A
        T-34/85 Model 1944   ** A

Zvezda T-34/76 Model 1942   *** B
1/25

Tamiya T-34/85 Model 1944   ** A

KEY

Symbol	Meaning
***	a top quality kit
**	medium quality
*	less detailed
A	simple enough for a beginner to build successfully
B	suitable for moderately experienced modellers
C	for experts only

Note: the marking of kits and accessories as simple enough for a beginner is not intended to devalue them in expert eyes, just to show which ones inexperienced modellers can tackle and still produce good results.

BELOW **Maquette of Russia has this neat T-35/85 with a late-production turret. It includes separate track links and a decal sheet with an enormous choice of markings. The only snag is that many of them belong on tanks with one of the other turrets or different wheels, but if you want to build a set of different T-35/85s it's worth looking for this kit so you can use its decals on them.**

Eduard also has four etched-metal sets for the T-34. One is for the Tamiya T-34/76 Model 1943, one for the Zvezda Model 1942, and two give exterior and interior parts for the RPM T-34/85. Rating *** B. If you can't find them locally, the UK agent is LSA Models, telephone 01273 705420, Email *lsamodels@mc.mail.com.*

Friulmodel makes a link-to-link white metal track set for the T-34. All their track sets were originally produced with jaws to be pressed close over pins cast into the next link, but now they are changing to a new style which uses pins cut from supplied wire to join the link. Both types are easy to use, but you should be aware that the early type can come stretch or undone under their own weight. Rating *** A. Available from Historex Agents in the UK.

Jaguar Models make a very nice fighting compartment interior set for the Dragon T-34/85 (see photo on page 58), which includes a complete turret with internal details, and also an engine set. Jaguar sets are sometimes hard to find in the UK, but can be ordered direct from them at 532 S. Coralridge Place, City of Industry, CA 91746, USA, website *www.jaguarmodels.com*, Email *sales@jaguarmodels.com.*

Jordi Rubio is an established maker of turned aluminium gun barrels, which simply replace the plastic parts, and produces one for the T-34/76 and one for the T-34/85. Rating *** A. They are available from LSA Models in the UK and from armour-model shops in the US and other countries.

Model Kasten of Japan also has link-to-link track sets for the T-34. These are in plastic and are easy to assemble. Three different types are available as working tracks, which can be built to remain flexible, and two as non-working tracks which must be cemented together in the shape they are to keep. Rating: *** A. Accurate Armour is the UK agent for Model Kasten.

RPM makes a basic engine and transmission set which fits any T-34 kit, and also sells as separate accessories the tracks and the turret of their T-34 kit. Rating ** A. Available wherever the RPM/Maquette T-34 is sold.

Tank Workshop has a range of resin sets for Tamiya's T-34 kits. These were previously available under the Tank Maker label but are being gradually repacked as Tank Workshop. It includes replacement wheels of various types and even complete replacement turrets. The wheels can be adapted to other kits, though the turrets may not be the right size to look right on some other maker's offerings. Rating *** A. Contact LSA Models in the UK for details of what is available in the UK. Tank Workshop products can be bought from good model shops in the USA where the range is made.

Verlinden Productions have a resin upgrade set to provide extra details and improved parts for the Tamiya T-34/85. They also make a rubdown decal set with T-34 markings. Rating *** B. Larger model shops often stock the Verlinden range, but you can also mail order from Historex Agents in the UK and from many stockists in other countries.

WORKING WITH MATERIALS OTHER THAN POLYSTYRENE

Etched-metal sets are usually in brass but may be nickel steel. Either is easy to work if you follow a few simple rules. Rest the metal fret on a hard surface and use a knife blade to cut the parts away, not scissors or side cutters which will tend to distort it. Use a 'spare' finger to hold down the part you're cutting as otherwise it can ping away and be hard to find. Similarly be careful with tweezers! For fixing etched-metal parts to your model you'll need either a two-part epoxy cement or superglue — if the joining surface is tiny the gel-type superglue works best. Use a wooden cocktail stick to put a blob of glue on the part and press it to the model — when the stick gets clogged up, just whittle away its end to reshape it.

Resin is equally easy to work with but its dust is dangerous to breathe, so a few simple precautions are needed. In the first place use a knife to cut away the casting blocks whenever you can; that way you create no dust. If you must saw, file or sandpaper away excess resin; use a dust mask, available from any DIY store. Sand with wet-and-dry paper used wet, to keep the dust down, and always dispose of the dust into a sealable plastic bag as soon as you can. The dust does have a practical use so keep a little in a tight-lidded pot. Resin parts can have small bubbles in them, created by gasses forming while the resin cures in its mould. These can often be filled by using modelling putty, but if they're on an edge or corner the best way to fill them is to put in a small blob of superglue and press a pinch of resin dust onto it. This will set like new resin, so you can carve it to shape and create a sharp edge without having your filler fall out. Epoxy glue or superglue are needed to fix resin parts in place.

White metal is used by some modellers. It is quite soft and easily bent or broken, so be gentle while you handle the parts. Mould seams or the remains of cut-away casting blocks are very easy to clean up with the edge of a blunt knife blade or with a file, and you can use the same epoxy glue or superglue to fix it.

REFERENCES

BIBLIOGRAPHY

There are two excellent T-34 reference books in the Osprey New Vanguard series. *New Vanguard 9, T-34/76 Medium Tank 1941-1945* by Steve Zaloga (Osprey, 1994, ISBN 1-85532-382-6) and *New Vanguard 20, T-34-85 Medium Tank 1944-1994* by Steve Zaloga and Jim Kinnear (Osprey, 1996, ISBN 1-85532-535-7) cover between them all the gun tank T-34s and their users as well as the self-propelled guns and recovery vehicles built on the same chassis. The different guns, turrets, wheels etc are described and illustrated, and both books have not only a good selection of wartime photographs showing the tanks in their service markings but also colour plates by Peter Sarson showing the colour schemes with more markings.

Another good reference is *T-34 In Action* by Steven Zaloga and James Grandsen (Squadron/Signal Publications, 1981, ISBN 0-89747-112-1). This one is more of a photobook with some supporting text, and as well as many in-service photographs of all the gun tanks it includes plans and sketches to show the different turrets etc. It also includes colour plates showing markings and camouflage schemes, and there is no overlap here with the New Vanguard titles.

These are the best English-language books on the T-34, though of course many photographs and details of its development can be found in more general books on Soviet tanks and on the Russian Front of World War II.

There are also quite a few Russian-language books on the T-34, and it is to be hoped that translations of some of them into English will eventually appear. Meanwhile one Russian book well worth looking at is *Camouflage of the Tanks of the Red Army 1930-1945* by Maxim Kolomietz and Ilya Moshchanskii (Armada-Vertical No 5,

1999, no ISBN). This is a photobook with many photographs and colour plates of T-34s as well as of other Soviet tanks, and the text and captions are in English. Several of the bookshops and the model shops which specialise in Eastern European models carry this in the UK and can be found by checking their advertisements in *Military Modelling* magazine, and a known stockist in the US is Eastern Front Models, PO Box 783 Madison, AL 35758, telephone (256) 971-1224, fax (256) 971-1688, Email *bob.lessels@mindspring.com*.

T-34s IN MUSEUMS

Preserved T-34/76s seem to be very rare birds, though several Model 1943s exist as War Memorials in Russia and Model 1941s are in the collection at Kubinka and another is at the Aberdeen Proving Ground in Maryland, USA. Unfortunately the former is not open to the general public. T-34/85s, on the other hand, can be found in most of the major tank museums as well as in many private collections. The Tank Museum at Bovington has one which was captured in Korea, and can be contacted at The Tank Museum, Bovington, Dorset, BH20 6JG, telephone 01929 405096, Email *admin@tankmuseum.co.uk*.

The Musée des Blindes at Saumur in France also has a T-34/85 and can be contacted at Musée des Blindes, 1043 route de Fontrevaud, 49000-Saumur, France, telephone 021 41 53 0699, Email *museedes-blindes@symphonie-fai.fr*.

In the USA there are several T-34/85s at the Patton Museum, PO Box 208, Fort Knox, KY 40121-0208, telephone (502) 624-3812, and — as already been said — the other major museums also have specimens.

ABOVE **This is a T-34/76 Model 1941 with a welded turret, a Model 1941 gun mantlet, mounted on a hull showing all the early characteristics — no mantlet for the hull machine gun, rounded front edge to the hull, and single driver's periscope instead of the double vision blocks with hinged covers fitted to later tanks.**

T-34 WEBSITES

At the time of writing no websites dedicated to the T-34 are known. However, there are several dedicated to Soviet military matters which includes much material on the T-34. One is Red Steel, at http://www.algonet.se/~toriert/introduction.htm, and it is written in English and well worth a visit. Another good site is the Russian Military Zone, also in English and to be found at http://www.history.enjoy.ru/index.html.

Apart from these there are useful tank discussion groups, where visitors are welcome to ask questions and get answers from armour enthusiasts including well-known modellers and armour experts. AFV News is at http://www.mo.money.com/AFV-news/, Missing Links at http://missing-lynx.com/, Track-Link at http://www.track-link.net/, and Hyperscale at http://www.hyperscale.com/. At these sites you can get help not only on the details of T-34s but also on the selection of the best kit for the model you want to build, and all apart from AFV News include pages with reviews of kits and accessories.

There are too many other tank discussion groups and reference sites for all to be listed here, but links to them can be found at Tony Matelliano's Scale Model Links, a superb site giving links to all kinds of modelling web resources at http://www.buffnet.net/~tonym/models.htm.

BELOW **Here's the Saumur T-34/76 Model 1942 showing the shape of its cast turret.**